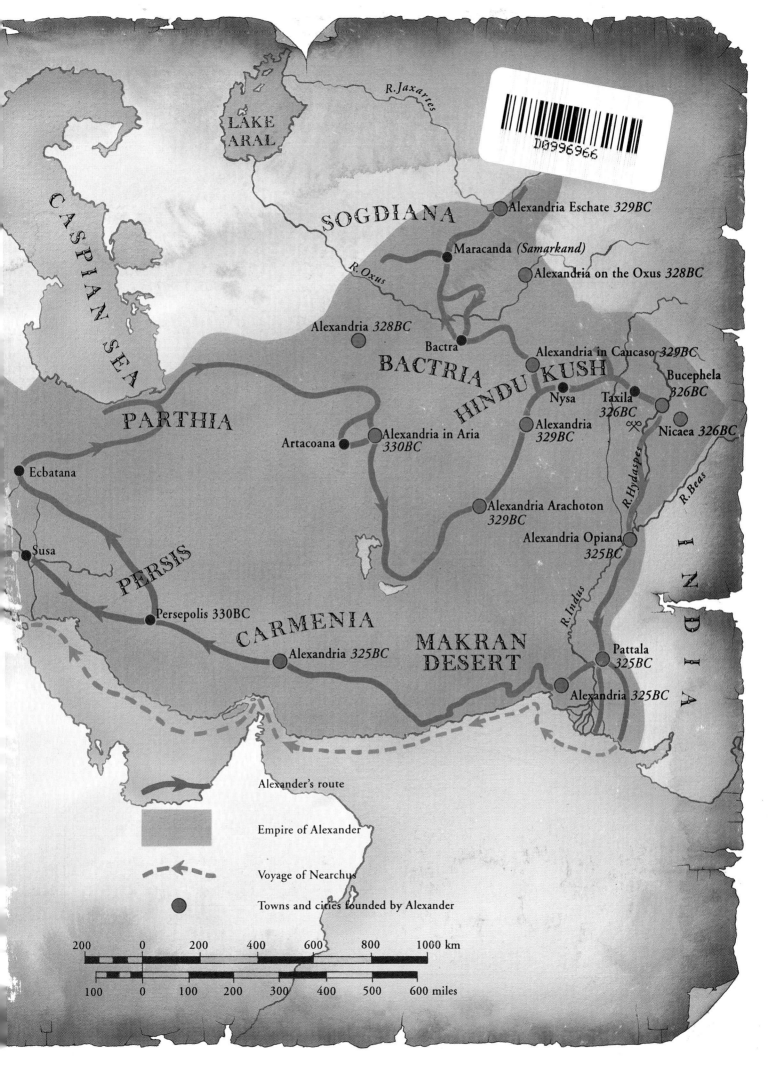

R.Jaxartes

LAKE
ARAL

SOGDIANA

Alexandria Eschate *329BC*

Maracanda *(Samarkand)*

R.Oxus

Alexandria on the Oxus *328BC*

CASPIAN SEA

Alexandria *328BC*

Bactra

BACTRIA

HINDU KUSH

Alexandria in Caucaso *329BC*

Nysa

Bucephela
326BC

Taxila
326BC

PARTHIA

Alexandria in Aria
330BC

Artacoana

Alexandria
329BC

Nicaea *326BC*

Ecbatana

R.Hydaspes

R.Beas

Alexandria Arachoton
329BC

Alexandria Opiana
325BC

Susa

PERSIS

INDIA

R.Indus

Persepolis 330BC

CARMENIA

MAKRAN
DESERT

Pattala
325BC

Alexandria *325BC*

Alexandria *325BC*

Alexander's route

Empire of Alexander

Voyage of Nearchus

Towns and cities founded by Alexander

| 200 | 0 | 200 | 400 | 600 | 800 | 1000 km |

| 100 | 0 | 100 | 200 | 300 | 400 | 500 | 600 miles |

WHO WAS
ALEXANDER
THE GREAT?

DAVID NASMYTH

ILLUSTRATED BY PETER DENNIS

First published in Great Britain 1998 by
Macdonald Young Books an imprint of
Wayland Publishers Ltd
61 Western Road
Hove
East Sussex BN3 1JD

Find Macdonald Young Books on the Internet at:
http://www.myb.co.uk

Series concept and text
© Wendy and Sally Knowles

Design and illustrations
© Macdonald Young Books

Edited by Wendy Knowles
Designed by Celia Hart
Series design by David Fordham
Map artist: Brett Breckon

Printed and bound in Portugal by Edições ASA

ISBN 07500 2272 8

The front cover portrait of Alexander the Great
is based on coins and statues from his reign.

Photograph acknowledgements:

We are grateful to the following for permission to
reproduce photographs:
Front Cover: The Bridgeman Art Library, (tr);
The British Museum, London, (tl) (1912.4-19.3);
E.T. Archive/Archaeological Museum, Sofia, (br);
E.T. Archive/Fitzwilliam Museum Cambridge, (bl).

AKG London, pages 10 (cl) (Bibliotheque
Nationale), 23 (National Museum of
Archaeology, Naples), 41 (t) (The British
Museum, London); Ashmolean Museum,
Oxford, page 25 (c); The Bridgeman Art Library,
pages 15 (r), 19 (t) and 38 (The Louvre, Paris),
25 (b) (The British Museum, London), 22 (t)
(Bonhams, London); The British Library,
London, page 36 (b) (AD 18804 f104r); The
British Museum, London, pages 9 (r) (1g 12.4-
19.3), 9 (l) (sculpture 869), 39 (t) (Ref 1910
11.5.33 c.101.14); C.M. Dixon, pages 19 (b), 21
(b), 22 (b), 30 (c), 32 (b) and 36 (t) (The British
Museum, London), E.T. Archive, pages 10 (t)
(Archaeological Museum, Dion, Greece), 10 (bl)
15 (l) and 39 (b) (Archaeological Museum,
Salonica, Greece), 16 (t) and 16 (b) (Pella
Museum, Greece), 25 (t) (Archaeological
Museum, Ferrara), 26 (Fitzwilliam Museum,
Cambridge, 29 (t) (British Museum, London),
29 (b), 30 (t) (Archaeological Museum, Sofia),
32 (t) (Villa Giulia Museum, Rome), 33, 35 (l);
Michael Holford, pages 11, 13 (t), 13 b), 35 (r)
and 37 (The British Museum, London)
Scala/National Museum, Napoli, page 12, 21 (t);
Ronald Sheridan/Ancient Art & Architecture,
pages 9 (a), 30 (b), 40, 41 (r); Spyros
Tsavdaroglou, page 14;

Picture Research by Valerie Mulcahy

CONTENTS

ALEXANDER'S GREECE

Alexander the Great became King of Macedonia, the most powerful state in Greece, in 336 BC. Within 13 years, and with an army of never more than 35,000 men, he had confirmed himself as master of Greece. He had also defeated the vast Persian empire, conquering territories in Asia Minor, Egypt and India. But Alexander was more than just a brilliant general. He was also a pupil of the famous Greek philosopher, Aristotle, and a lover of Greek drama and literature. His conquests were responsible for spreading Greek thought and culture throughout Egypt, northern India, central Asia and the eastern Mediterranean.

WHAT WAS ALEXANDER'S GREECE LIKE?

Ancient Greece was never one united country but made up of a number of small, independent states. Competition between these states for land and trade was fierce. Two of the most powerful states, Athens and Sparta, fought a long and bloody war, known as the Peloponnesian War. It lasted for 27 years (431–404 BC). But in 338 BC, a small, northern Greek kingdom called Macedonia smashed the joint army of the other Greek states at the Battle of Chaeronea and became the most powerful state in Greece.

MACEDONIA
Cut off from the rest of the Greek world by its geographical position, it had managed to avoid getting involved in the long, drawn-out Peloponnesian War that had devastated Greece.

This portrait of Alexander is based upon a famous sculpture in the Louvre Museum, Paris. One of the greatest generals the world has ever known, Alexander was only 32 when he died in 323 BC.

A coin of a Macedonian horsemen. Like the city-states of southern Greece, such as Athens and Sparta, the people of this wild, mountainous kingdom spoke Greek.

WHAT WAS SPECIAL ABOUT THE MACEDONIAN STYLE OF GOVERNMENT?

There was a strong tradition of the king consulting his subjects. This arose from the king's habit of going out on hunting parties with his closest companions, where all were thought to be equal. Another tradition that set Macedonian government apart was toleration. Macedonia did not humiliate a defeated opponent. Once a victory was gained, the Macedonians looked at how they could get the defeated people to collaborate with them. All of these traditions were to stand Alexander in good stead when he was building up his empire.

A bronze arrow-head bearing the name of Philip of Macedonia in Classical Greek. Philip's right eye had been cut out by an arrow as he inspected his troops' catapults outside the walls of a besieged city.

HOW DID MACEDONIA COME TO BE SO POWERFUL?

The weakness of the other Greek states after the long war coincided with the time when Macedonia was ruled by a very strong king named Philip II. Macedonian kings had lots of power, most of the state taxes went to the king. He could use this money to build ships or pay for a professional army. Philip made the Macedonian army the most powerful army in Greece.

Troops besieging a 4th-century Greek city. The weakness of the other Greek states after the long Peloponnesian War gave Philip of Macedonia the opportunity to make himself master of Greece.

BEGINNINGS

On the night of 20 July, 356 BC, the rich and famous temple of the goddess, Artemis, burnt down in the Greek city of Ephesus. Word soon went round that this was the will of the gods, who had struck the temple with a flash of lightning, because a child had been born that day who would become the master of all the world. That same night, Alexander the Great was born.

A gold crown of ivy leaves from a tomb in northern Greece. A similar wreath was found in the tomb of Philip of Macedonia. Philip's conquest of the gold mines of Thrace helped pay for his expansion plans.

A gold portrait of Alexander's father, Philip II. A remarkable man, he created the professional army that helped to make Alexander's victories possible later.

DID PHILIP LAY THE FOUNDATIONS FOR ALEXANDER'S SUCCESS?

Under his leadership Macedonia's boundaries were more than doubled. A brilliant military commander, he created the disciplined, professional army – particularly the cavalry section – that helped to make Alexander's victories possible later on. The main weapon used by his soldiers was the sarissa, a long spear. Men armed with sarissas did not need to wear heavy armour. They could fight at long range, march fast and manoeuvre easily.

WHO WERE HIS PARENTS?

Philip II, the king of Macedonia, and his wife Olympias. Intelligent and energetic, Philip's ambition was to extend the boundaries of his kingdom, even as far away as Persia. Olympias was a princess from Epirus, to the west of Macedonia, who worshipped snakes and played with them in religious ceremonies.

Alexander's mother, Olympias. She had a fiery temper and would stop at nothing to get what she wanted. Alexander was very like her.

Through his mother, Olympias, Alexander could supposedly trace his ancestry back to the Greek mythical hero, Achilles. On his father's side he claimed to be descended from the Greek hero, Hercules, and from Zeus, the father of the gods.

WHAT WAS PHILIP OF MACEDONIA'S COURT LIKE?

As Philip's military successes grew, and Macedonia became more wealthy, his court at Pella attracted experts from all over the Greek world – doctors, engineers, philosophers and architects as well as actors, artists and musicians. Here, the young Alexander and his friends would have come into contact with a much wider world than that of Macedonia.

Remains of the royal palace at Pella (left). At Philip's court, Alexander listened to Greek plays and poems and developed his love of Greek culture.

Alexander and his father watch Philip's troops. Throughout his life, Alexander needed to show that he was better than his father. If his father was a hero, he was going to be a super-hero.

ALEXANDER'S CHILDHOOD

Philip intended Alexander to follow him as king of Macedonia from the moment he was born and Alexander's whole childhood was a preparation for this.

Alexander being taught by Aristotle. Like most wealthy Greek boys Alexander would have learnt reading, writing, public speaking and music.

Aristotle, Alexander's teacher, believed that Greeks were superior to other nations, whom they called barbarians. Barbarians, he said, were natural slaves and inferiors.

DID HE GO TO SCHOOL?

As the son of a king, Alexander would have been taught in the palace by tutors.

Philip of Macedonia was very keen that his son should be well-educated. In 343 or 342 BC he engaged a man called Aristotle as his teacher. A pupil of the great Greek philosopher, Plato, Aristotle was the most famous intellectual figure of his time.

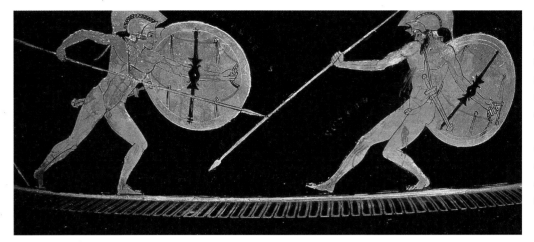

A scene from the Iliad on a Greek vase showing the combat between Achilles (left) and Hector. Alexander modelled himself on Achilles. He took his copy of the Iliad with him on all his adventures until the day he died. He used to sleep with a dagger and his book beneath his head.

WHAT DID ARISTOTLE TEACH ALEXANDER?

He taught him about the countries of the earth, as far east even as India, and the lands of the midnight sun which no Greek had ever seen. Alexander made up his mind to go there. Aristotle taught him about the Greek heroes of old who fought around the great city of Troy. He gave Alexander a copy of a book by the Greek poet, Homer, all about these heroes. It had Aristotle's own notes written in the margins. The book was called the *Iliad* and it made Alexander decide to become a hero. Aristotle believed that Greeks were superior to the nations around them, whom they called barbarians. He probably taught Alexander this.

WHAT ELSE DID HE LEARN?

Alexander would have been taught physical exercise. One day a special horse was brought to him by his father. The horse was large and strong, black, but with a white mark on his forehead like the head of an ox. He would throw off anyone who tried to mount him, and trample on them. Alexander noticed something about the horse: whenever he saw his own shadow, he was frightened and grew angry. So he turned the horse towards the sun, where he could not see his shadow, and started to ride him.

Alexander called his black horse Bucephalus (which means ox-head), and Bucephalus went with Alexander on all his travels, even as far away as India.

When Philip saw Alexander riding the black horse, he said to him, 'Son, you had better find a new kingdom of your own to rule over, because Macedonia will not be big enough for you as well as me'.

DEATH OF PHILIP OF MACEDONIA

Philip's long-term plan was always to build up an empire in Asia and attack the Persian king. In order to do this he needed to conquer the other Greek states and unite them under his command. His victory at Chaeronea achieved this.

A carved ivory head, thought to be of Philip II, found in his tomb.

WAS ALEXANDER INVOLVED IN PHILIP'S CAMPAIGNS?

As he grew up, Alexander was entrusted with more and more command by his father. He showed every sign of being a brilliant commander. Already, when only 18, he had led the cavalry charge at the Battle of Chaeronea in 338 BC. But the king always needed to watch him, because Philip's relations with Olympias, Alexander's mother, were getting worse. She was very ambitious for her son, and Philip began to feel that she was a threat.

WHAT DID PHILIP DECIDE TO DO?

In 337 BC, Philip was at the height of his power. He announced that he would divorce Alexander's mother, Olympias, and take another queen, the young daughter of a Macedonian noble. Alexander was furious, but he could do nothing about it. However his luck altered. In October 336 BC, Philip was murdered at an enormous banquet held to celebrate the marriage of his daughter to the King of Epirus.

A gold quiver was found in the tomb of Philip II, decorated with scenes from the capture of a city.

Alexander buries his father, Philip in a magnificent tomb. When archaeologists found the tomb at Vergina in 1976, there inside were all Philip's gold and silver treasures, exactly as Alexander had left them.

WHO KILLED PHILIP?

Members of the king's bodyguard, who had a grudge and felt taken for granted. Alexander's mother, Olympias, almost certainly knew about the plot, and encouraged it. Alexander wasn't involved – it would have been too risky, as well as dishonourable. Alexander always hated ingratitude, and this action would have been unacceptable to him. However, he had to act fast to safeguard his position as heir. He was at once presented to the army as king. After it had accepted him there were speedy executions of all those who had previously questioned his position as heir.

A gold casket from Philip II's tomb, decorated with the star emblem of the Macedonian kings.

HOW DID ALEXANDER REACT TO HIS FATHER'S DEATH?

He probably felt grief, mixed with a feeling of relief that he was now king. He immediately buried his father in a magnificent tomb, which he filled with Philip's armour and favourite possessions. The tomb was covered over with earth, and went unnoticed until 1976, when archaeologists found it.

ALEXANDER, THE YOUNG KING

Alexander knew that he was destined to conquer empires. His mother, Olympias, had put the idea into his head that he was more than human. All his life he aspired to be like Achilles, the Greek hero of Homer's poem, the *Iliad*.

WHAT DID HE LOOK LIKE?

Like his father, Philip, Alexander was rather short, but he made up for this by having great strength and energy. People who knew him noticed how he had eyes of different colours, one blue and one light brown, and his hair was fair, growing thickly over his head like the mane of a lion. His stare could be terrifying. You would not have wanted to make an enemy of him.

A marble head of Alexander as a young man – this is the most famous Alexander portrait, with a slight turn of the head, eyes looking upward, and hair swept up at the centre.

A pebble mosaic from Pella showing Alexander (left), wearing a traditional Macedonian hat, being rescued from a lion by his friend, Craterus.

WHO WERE HIS FRIENDS?

He had a close circle of friends to whom he told his secrets and they would gladly have given their lives for him. They included Hephaestion, who had been a childhood friend at his father's court in Pella, and was his closest companion, and Ptolemy, who later became Ptolemy I, King of Egypt. When Hephaestion died prematurely in 324 BC, Alexander was overwhelmed with grief (see page 38).

HOW DID HE RELAX?

Alexander's idea of enjoyment was to go on long hunting trips or fighting against the tribes on the borders of his kingdom. He was also one of the first people in the Ancient World to read 'silently'. That may seem quite strange to us, but most people in the Ancient World read out loud. The art of memory was very highly prized. The works of poets and even of historians were designed to be read aloud.

Alexander and his friends hunting wild boar. Philip had decreed that the sons of Macedonian nobles should be educated as pages at Pella. Later, a number of these boyhood friends were to become members of Alexander's personal bodyguard.

THEBES AND THE PUSH TOWARDS PERSIA

One of Alexander's first acts as king was to attack the city-state of Thebes, which had been the centre of resistance towards Philip. He captured it in September 335 BC, and gave orders for it to be destroyed. Only one house was left standing: the house of a poet called Pindar, which Alexander wanted spared, because he had heard about Pindar from his teacher, Aristotle. After this, most of the Greek states surrendered to him. Alexander now turned his face towards Persia. This great empire ruled all of the east. Many years before Alexander, the Persians had even invaded Greece and burnt its temples.

Like his father, Philip, Alexander was determined to attack Persia and build up an empire in the east.

WHAT WAS ALEXANDER'S FIRST MOVE?

Quickly he gathered together an army. In the spring of 334 BC, Alexander was twenty-one. Dressed in his golden armour, he crossed the Hellespont, (the narrow stretch of water which separates Europe from the vast continent of Asia). Next he went to Troy to make a sacrifice to the spirits of the heroes of the *Iliad*.

Crossing the waters of the Hellespont, Alexander steered the royal trireme (ship) himself. The first to leap from the bows of the ship, he is supposed to have flung his spear into the soil of Asia to claim it as 'spear-won ground'.

An enamelled brick frieze of Persian archers. Whatever Alexander's teacher, Aristotle might have taught him about the Persians being barbarians and inferiors, they were still the greatest power in the world.

A Greek vase painting (below) showing Achilles binding the wounds of his friend. After the Battle of Granicus, Alexander visited his men one by one, showed them his own wounds, and rewarded them richly.

HOW DID THE PERSIANS REACT TO THIS INVASION?

Alexander had enough food and money to feed his men for only a few months, and the Persians could have starved him out, but the Persian officers were gentlemen who believed in giving a fair fight. So they sent a relatively small force to meet him, in May, 334 BC, near a river called the Granicus (which is in modern Turkey).

Alexander is the first to leap from the ship. He never asked his men to do anything he wouldn't do himself.

WHAT HAPPENED AT THE BATTLE OF GRANICUS?

Before the Persians were ready for him, Alexander charged across the river at its shallowest point and attacked their general. The Persians fled, and Alexander was victorious, at least for the time being. But the Persians were not foolish; they wanted to choose their own battleground and sent spies to watch Alexander's movements.

ON THROUGH THE CITIES OF ASIA MINOR

After his decisive victory at the Granicus, Alexander then proceeded to conquer the coastal cities of Asia Minor (modern Turkey). Alexander knew that these cities had to be held to prevent the Persians using them for a counter-attack in the Aegean Sea while he was moving inland. In one of them, a queen called Ada presented Alexander with a marvellous tray of sweets and cakes. Alexander was so amused by this that he let her continue to be queen, and said she was like a second mother to him.

At the city of Gordium there was a famous chariot tied with a knot that no one had ever been able to untie. Alexander took his sword and cut through it. When somebody acts very decisively, we call this 'cutting the Gordian knot'.

At the battle of Issus, Alexander, (shown left in this mosaic) faced a huge army formed from all the countries of the Persian empire, led by the Persian king, Darius himself (in the chariot). He knew that if he could drive Darius away the Persian army would collapse in chaos.

COULD THE PERSIANS STOP ALEXANDER?

They certainly thought they could. After a full year of campaigning, Alexander's force was short of food. Their only hope was to cross the narrow mountain pass which separates modern Turkey from Syria, and go down to the fertile plains of Syria. It was here in November, 333 BC, that a huge Persian army led by King Darius himself, finally caught up with Alexander at Issus.

WAS HE IN SERIOUS DANGER?

Yes. He was trapped between the mountains and the sea, by an army that outnumbered his by more than five to one. Few of Alexander's men slept easily that night; they were too afraid. They needn't have worried. Alexander had a plan. The following morning he revealed his scheme to his troops; it was to make a straight attack against the Persian king.

WHAT WAS THE OUTCOME AT ISSUS?

At first the battle went badly for Alexander, but at the crucial moment he succeeded in breaking through the enemy ranks with a small force of expert cavalry. When Darius saw this he began to fight bravely, but then he fled on his chariot, and the Persians were left without a commander. By the end of the day they had all been killed or surrendered.

A detail from the famous 'Alexander Sarcophagus' showing Alexander, wearing the lion helmet of Hercules, on his horse Bucephalus at the battle of Issus.

The Macedonian attack at Issus was launched, as always, by Alexander at the head of his cavalry.

GENEROUS IN VICTORY

Alexander was always generous to his vanquished opponents if they surrendered honourably. But if they cheated him, or refused to surrender, he would show no mercy.

WHAT HAPPENED TO THE DEFEATED PERSIANS?

After the battle of Issus Alexander and his men found a splendid tent, inside which were the wife and mother of Darius. Alexander went into the tent accompanied by Hephaestion, his closest friend and second-in-command. The royal ladies turned to Hephaestion, thinking that he was Alexander, because he was so much taller than his master. Hephaestion told them that they were making a mistake, but Alexander said, 'Ladies, do not worry, because he is an Alexander too'. Unlike some leaders, Alexander was never jealous of his friends. Also, his treatment of the captured women shows the respect he held for them. Perhaps he was beginning to realise that barbarians could be human too.

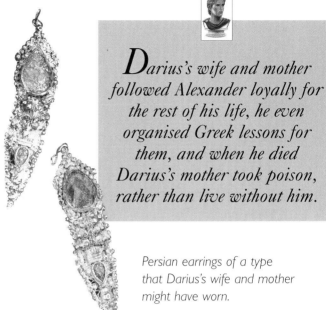

Darius's wife and mother followed Alexander loyally for the rest of his life, he even organised Greek lessons for them, and when he died Darius's mother took poison, rather than live without him.

Persian earrings of a type that Darius's wife and mother might have worn.

DID ALEXANDER CAPTURE THE PERSIAN KING, DARIUS?

No. The story goes that after his failed pursuit of Darius, Alexander returned to camp and decided to take a wash in Darius's bath. Inside Darius's tent Alexander found golden cups, bowls, pitchers and caskets of gold. When he saw these exquisitely worked treasures, Alexander looked long at his friends and remarked, 'This, it would seem, is to be a king'. Afterwards he was to keep his precious copy of Homer's *Iliad* in Darius's casket.

A gold model of a chariot from the Oxus treasure. Inside the chariot sits a Persian prince. The River Oxus is in northern Afghanistan – this shows how far the ancient Persian empire extended.

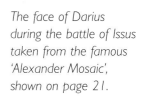

HOW DID DARIUS REACT TO HIS DEFEAT?

About this time Alexander received a letter from Darius, which went like this. 'I see that the gods have favoured you, Alexander; but do not be too proud of yourself. You can keep the western half of my empire, if you agree to stop fighting me and live in peace.' Alexander replied without delay. 'King, you offer me half your empire, but you are only giving me something I already have. I am on my way to take the other half too, and be sure that, wherever you hide, I will come and seek you out.'

The face of Darius during the battle of Issus taken from the famous 'Alexander Mosaic', shown on page 21.

Darius's offer appealed to Alexander's elderly second-in-command, Parmenion, who said, 'I would accept if I were Alexander.' Alexander replied, 'So would I, if I were Parmenion.'

Darius flees the battle of Issus in his chariot, leaving the Persians without a commander. By the end of the day they had all been killed or surrendered and Darius had vanished.

ALEXANDER, THE GENERAL

The sheer variety of the obstacles that he had to overcome, and his speed and decisiveness, even when hopelessly outnumbered show that Alexander was truly a great general.

HOW DID HE WIN HIS BATTLES?

An account of Macedonian troops written at the time describes a typical battle strategy of his. 'Alexander drew up his army with the phalanx, 16 men deep. On each flank was a force of 200 cavalry. He ordered them all to keep quiet, so they could pick up the words of command quickly. The first order he gave was to the infantry to raise their spears upright and then bring them 'to the ready' at the word of command. Then they were to swing their massed points in a tight body now to the right and now to the left. Also, Alexander moved the phalanx smartly forward and then kept changing direction. Now he wheeled to one flank, now to the other. In this way he went through many movements and changes of formation within a short time.'

Alexander reviews a typical battle formation. In the centre were the infantry armed with their famous sarissas or long spears. Terrified opponents compared the effect to spikes on a giant porcupine.

WAS ALEXANDER BRAVE?

Unquestionably. He led from the front and was always in the thick of the fighting. He wanted to show his men that he wasn't afraid to face the same danger as them. After a battle Alexander would visit all of his men. If any of them had been wounded he would talk to them so that they felt better and show them his own wounds. He never lost a battle, and he radiated confidence. He was able to succeed because his men were devoted to him and believed in him totally.

A detail from a painted pot showing a Greek warrior with a spear.

A type of helmet worn by Alexander's soldiers (above). This helmet was found in the River Tigris, possibly left by one of Alexander's soldiers.

WHAT DID HE DO WITH THE LANDS HE HAD CONQUERED?

He would put governors in to hold the territory until he returned. Sometimes he let local rulers, such as Queen Ada, continue to rule if he trusted them. Alexander could form an instant opinion about what a person was worth, regardless of whether they were Greek or barbarian. He was almost always right. But if that person once let him down, they could expect no mercy.

Stone frieze showing heavily armed Greek soldiers marching. Alexander's well-trained troops were totally devoted to him and quick to obey his commands.

ALEXANDER, THE GOD-KING IN EGYPT

After defeating the Persians at Issus, Alexander went on to Egypt. The Egyptians welcomed him with open arms as a liberator from the rule of the Persians and hailed him as pharaoh or king of Egypt. While he was in Egypt he spotted a place with a fine harbour, which he said he would turn into a great city. He gave orders for the city to be built and named it after himself – Alexandria. It is still one of the biggest cities in Egypt.

A silver coin, showing Alexander wearing the ram's horns, the symbol of the Egyptian god, Ammon.

HOW DID EGYPT AFFECT ALEXANDER?

Almost his first act while in Egypt was to go on a journey far into the desert, to an oasis called Siwa. Here, there was a temple of a god named Ammon, whom the Greeks equated with their god, Zeus. People believed that Ammon's image could tell the future, and Alexander wanted to know what was in store for him. He was very superstitious, like his mother, and like many soldiers who risk their lives everyday.

WHAT DID THE GOD TELL HIM?

The image of the god was carried by priests and answered questions by weighing on the priests' shoulders one way or another. The god told him many things, but above all that King Philip had never been Alexander's father. It said that his real father was the god Ammon himself and that Alexander would conquer the whole world. Everyone agreed that after this meeting Alexander was a changed person: his pride and selfishness began to grow, and he started to drink too much wine.

The Greek historian, Plutarch, tells the story that the intended greeting of the priests was 'child', in Greek, 'paidios,' and that Alexander thought they said, 'pai Dios,' 'son of Zeus'.

THE STORY OF ALEXANDER'S VISIT TO SIWA

*N*o *one knows for sure what the god really said to Alexander. He never revealed what he had asked, but according to his historian, Callisthenes, 'he used to say that he had heard what pleased him'. After his visit to Siwa, Alexander believed more and more that he was a god.*

Alexander visits the temple of Ammon at Siwa.

RULER OF PERSIA

Alexander wasn't satisfied with ruling Egypt. On he went, east, crossing the Eastern Desert and the Euphrates and Tigris Rivers, towards Persia, hunting for the Persian king, Darius. At last he found him and a vast army, in the plains of what is now modern Iraq.

Alexander's men await the Persian chariot attack at the Battle of Gaugamela.

WAS DARIUS EXPECTING ALEXANDER?

Yes. He had learnt from the battles of Granicus and Issus and was determined not to be caught out this time. He prepared extensively for the battle, equipping his cavalry with the large swords and short thrusting spears of the Macedonians, and working out a battle plan to cope with Alexander's usual battle formation. He had chosen the battle site at Gaugamela with great care. He had even gone to the trouble of having the battlefield levelled to make it easy for his 200 chariots to attack. Now all he had to do was wait for Alexander and wipe him out.

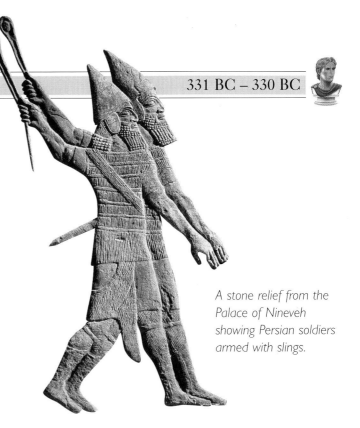

WHO WON THE BATTLE OF GAUGAMELA?

Some days before the battle there was an eclipse of the moon, which frightened Alexander's troops and horses. But Alexander said that it was a sign, sent by the gods, that the power of Persia was at an end. On October 1, 331 BC, the morning of the battle, to the anxiety of his generals Alexander was late getting up. He had been working long into the night on a brilliant battleplan designed for an outnumbered defence. It paid off. The vast Persian army was defeated, and Darius fled.

A stone relief from the Palace of Nineveh showing Persian soldiers armed with slings.

The historian, Arrian, reports that Darius had an unbelievable total of 400,000 horsemen. It would have been much less, but still probably five times more men than Alexander.

WHAT HAPPENED TO DARIUS?

One of Darius's governors caught up with him near the mountains and killed him. He thought that this would please Alexander, but Alexander had the governor put to death for doing such an evil thing to his own king. Now Alexander had no rival. He could seize control of the vast Persian empire. From now on he acted as King of Persia, and to win the support of the Persian aristocracy he appointed many Persians as provincial governors.

A stone relief showing a procession of nobles in the palace at Persepolis, the capital of the Persian kings. After the battle, the palace was burned down, perhaps on Alexander's orders.

TOO MUCH POWER?

After his defeat of the Persian king, Alexander was ruler of a vast empire and you would have thought that he had achieved his dream. However, he dreamed of being king of all Asia. But things were starting to change...

A silver drinking horn in the shape of a bull. Such horns would have been used at Macedonian drinking parties and on the night Cleitus died.

WHAT HAD CHANGED?

Alexander's officers had always felt able to speak freely to him. Cleitus, a brave officer who had saved Alexander's life at the battle of Granicus, voiced a grievance at a banquet in the city of Samarkand in central Asia, in 329 BC. But this time Alexander, who had drunk too much, threw his spear at him, killing Cleitus.

HOW HAD CLEITUS OFFENDED ALEXANDER?

Cleitus had said, 'Alexander, you used to be a soldier like us, but now you behave like the King of Persia you replaced'. He had offended Alexander because he had dared to criticise him, but also because Alexander was forced to ask himself if the Persians were his defeated enemies, or his partners in a new world.

A glazed brick frieze depicting a lion on a gateway in Babylon, one of the capitals of the Persian kings.

A stone relief from Persepolis showing gifts and tribute being brought to the Persian king.

Alexander's leadership was based upon a Macedonian tradition of close personal loyalty to the king, in which the king ate and drank with his men on equal terms. The Persian court was very different.

DID HE REGRET KILLING CLEITUS?

Yes. When he realised what he had done he broke down in tears, and had to be taken to his tent under guard. He wept bitterly for the next three days, because of what he had done to his friend. Many of his soldiers heard what had happened and became afraid. Whereas previously they had always felt able to speak their minds freely to him, now they dared not. However, they knew that without Alexander's leadership they wouldn't be able to get back to Macedonia.

Alexander kills his friend, Cleitus, in a fit of rage. Many of Alexander's men now feared him.

ALEXANDER IN INDIA

Alexander crossed the mountains into India, which he was determined to add to his empire. India was full of dangers: mighty warriors braver than the Persians, blistering heat, torrential rains known as monsoons, and elephants which the Indians used in battle and which terrified the Greeks' horses.

An early 3rd-century clay dish, showing an elephant equipped with a tower for bearing soldiers.

WHAT HAPPENED TO HIM IN INDIA?

At one point, an Indian tribe took refuge on top of the mountain of Pir-Sar which was so steep they thought nobody except them could climb it. Alexander and a crack troop of his men found a secret way up the mountain, and captured the Indians on the top. In one Indian city Alexander was wounded by an arrow, which pierced his chest and almost killed him.

HOW DID ALEXANDER REACT TO HIS NEAR-DEATH?

The story goes that news reached his army that he was dead. However, he recovered and arrived back at his camp by boat. Disembarking, he brushed aside all offers of a litter (chair) to carry him and insisted on mounting his horse and riding back into the camp. A round of applause broke through the entire army. He then approached his tent and dismounted so that everyone could see him walking too.

A Persian painting depicting a priestess beseeching Alexander not to destroy an Indian idol.

While in India they found a wise man, who had no belongings and spent his time thinking about the gods. He told Alexander that war was wrong and conquering people was a waste of effort. Alexander would not listen to him. Finally the Indian burnt himself alive on a fire, as a protest against what Alexander was doing.

WAS HIS INDIAN CAMPAIGN SUCCESSFUL?

In the short term it was very successful, but he could not have held on to all of India. In modern terms his conquests were confined to Pakistan, which the Greeks counted as part of India. Of the many rajahs or kings he encountered, the most powerful was Porus, whom he defeated at the Battle of Hydaspes in 326 BC. He was so impressed by Porus that later he made him governor of all parts of India that he had conquered. Alexander recognised that this barbarian was as good a warrior as he was.

His faithful horse, Bucephalus died shortly after the Battle of Hydaspes, and Alexander founded a city, Bucephala, on the spot where the horse was buried.

The Porus medallion (left) shows Alexander riding the ageing Bucephalus, attacking Porus on his elephant.

The Indian king, Porus, rides his elephant at the Battle of Hydaspes. Afterwards, Alexander sent an interpreter to ask Porus how he wished to be treated. 'Like a king,' he replied.

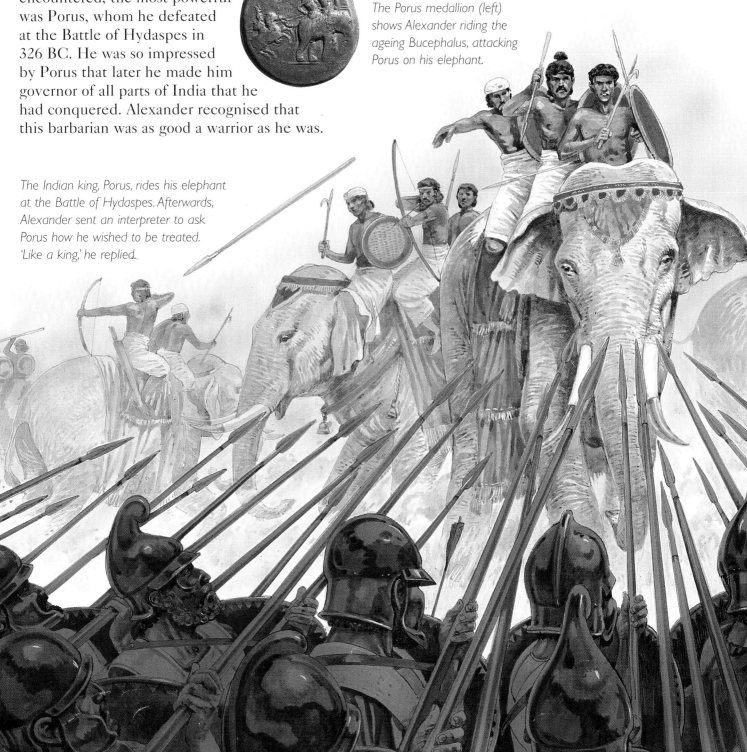

ENOUGH IS ENOUGH

Finally, in the summer of 325 BC, Alexander's men had had enough. There were legends of rich kingdoms to the east, but the monsoons had started. A rumour went round that they were nearing the ends of the earth, which they thought was flat, and they might fall off if they went any further.

HOW DID ALEXANDER DEAL WITH THIS?

He told his men to continue – all the way to China! But they refused. It was the only time his men ever said no him. Furious, he marched half of his army back to Persia, across the burning wilderness of the Makran Desert, where many of them died. He sent the rest back by ship, led by his admiral, Nearchus.

WHAT HAPPENED WHEN HE GOT BACK TO PERSIA?

He found his control over the heart of his empire weakened by his years of absence. Over the winter of 325 to 324 BC he executed and replaced several of his governors and senior officers. Throughout his empire there was a mood of fear and uncertainty.

Alexander's men cross the burning wastes of the Makran Desert on their journey home to Persia. Alexander had hoped to reach Ocean, the great mythical water that the Greeks believed encircled the world.

He was a born leader, and he was successful. Many of his men were volunteers and those who did not want to fight could go home. Life on the trail with Alexander would have been tough but interesting. The excitement of conquering an empire and the riches that came with it more than made up for all the hardships.

A stone relief (left) from Persepolis, of a camel with a bell, led by an envoy to the Persian king. These animals would have been used for Alexander's baggage train.

It took 60 days for his army to cross the Makran Desert. Some sources suggest that he lost three-quarters of his army.

A stone relief showing a Greek soldier fighting a 'barbarian'.

Many thousands. But unlike the Roman general Julius Caesar, he never killed people that surrendered to him. He saw war as a kind of sport – rather like two teams playing against each other. There were rules, and if you broke those rules then you would be treated differently.

THE CONQUEROR AND GREEK CULTURE

Alexander was proud to be Greek, as Aristotle had taught him. On his long march he took Greek scientists and architects with him, and he was keen to spread Greek ideas thoughout his empire. One way of doing that was to found cities along the routes of his campaigns. Although many of these were little more than military garrisons in the conquered territories, others maintained themselves as centres of Greek culture for generations.

Trumpeters were a feature at Greek feasts.

HOW DID HE REGARD THE DIFFERENT PEOPLES OF HIS EMPIRE?

He took the view that they were too many to be treated as enemies all the time, so perhaps they could be turned into allies. One way of doing that was to encourage his soldiers to take foreign wives and for the children of those marriages to be brought up in the Greek tradition. Back in central Asia, in 327 BC, he had selected a foreign wife for himself, a young princess named Roxane, from the country we now call Afghanistan. On his return to Susa in Persia in 324 BC, Alexander told 91 of his officers to marry 91 daughters of the Persian nobility, so that the old enemies, Greece and Persia would learn to understand each other. He himself took two more Persian wives. Any children of these marriages would be brought up to speak Greek and would be loyal, both to their own traditions, and to the culture of their conquerors.

The story of Alexander's life inspired artists from many cultures long after his death. He is shown here in an Indian painting depicting his wedding to Roxane.

WERE HIS OFFICERS HAPPY TO MARRY PERSIANS?

Each couple was given rich presents by Alexander, and they feasted for days. However some of his officers were unhappy about being told what to do in this way. They did not like being a part of his plans for introducing Greek culture to faraway peoples. They wanted to remain separate from them. But Alexander knew that this was impossible. The way forward had to be co-operation with the Persians, not constant hostility.

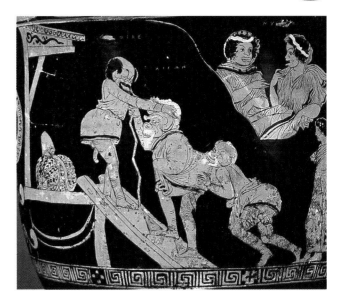

At the Susa wedding feasts, Greek tragedies and comedies were performed by Alexander's favourite Greek actors. These are Greek comic actors.

Alexander and 91 of his officers take Persian brides.

DID ALEXANDER REALISE HIS MEN WERE UNHAPPY?

Probably not – he hated ingratitude, and by now, his men would have tried to hide their feelings from him. He thought that all of his plans were going to work. If his men listened to him, they were going to be rulers of the earth. But his men were starting to think otherwise. They thought that he would never stop.

A TIME TO DIE

In the autumn of 324 BC, Alexander's boyhood friend, Hephaestion, died. He was possibly the only person Alexander had ever really loved. Grief-stricken, he returned to the city of Babylon (in modern Iraq), which he intended to make his capital. He had more plans, to conquer Arabia and Italy and Spain, but it was not to be.

HOW DID ALEXANDER DIE?

One day he went boating on a lake near the city, and the gold ribbon which was round his head blew away in the wind and settled on an old ruined building, which a priest told him was the grave of an ancient king. Everyone knew that this was a bad sign. A day or two later he fell ill with a fever, and began to grow weaker. As he lay on his bed in the palace all his soldiers filed past him, one by one. He recognised them all, but could not speak. On 10 June, 323 BC, he died, at the age of only thirty-two.

A marble head of Alexander. He was only thirty-two when he died.

HAD HE BEEN MURDERED?

Some said that he had been poisoned, but he was really worn out by years of marching and fighting, and the fever did the rest. His men were both dumbfounded and grief-stricken by his death. They were also frightened for the future because although his wife, Roxane, was expecting a child, there was no heir.

The marshes surrounding the lake on which Alexander went boating were infested with mosquitos. It is likely that Alexander's last illness was malaria.

WHAT HAPPENED TO HIS HUGE EMPIRE?

It soon fell to pieces after his death, with his generals fighting each other for the next 20 years for what was left of it, since none of them was as good a soldier as Alexander. As for what happened to his child by Roxane, we do not know for sure. But next to the tomb of Philip of Macedonia, there is also the tomb of a boy aged 16. He is almost certainly Alexander IV of Macedonia, the son of Alexander the Great and Roxane.

A coin issued by Alexander's successor in Macedonia, Cassander. It shows the idealised head of Alexander as a god. Cassander had Roxane and her young son, Alexander, killed.

One of Alexander's enemies in Greece commented on hearing of his death that he could not be dead because if he was dead the whole world would smell of his body!

A marble statue of a Macedonian foot soldier, armed with a sarissa and wearing the traditional Macedonian hat, found in the tomb of Philip II of Macedonia.

BURIED IN AFRICA

Alexander's body was placed in a golden carriage, with the intention of taking it back to Macedonia. But Ptolemy, one of his generals, hijacked it and carried it to Egypt, to the new city of Alexandria which Alexander had founded. There, where the two great streets of the city crossed each other, he was laid to rest in a huge marble monument. Perhaps he is still there, but we do not know, because no one has ever found him. So it happened that Alexander was born in Europe, died in Asia, and was eventually buried in Africa.

A 15th-century medieval manuscript, the 'Romance of Alexander', depicting him living in a submarine under the sea. Such was the fascination of Alexander to people that stories about his miraculous exploits continued to be told long after his death.

HOW WAS ALEXANDER REMEMBERED?

His empire soon collapsed, but he lived on in legend. Stories about him are found in Greek, Egyptian, Arabic (he appears in the Quran), Persian and some of the Indian languages, even in Chinese. In some of these tales he conquers the air by training eagles to pull him through the sky, and he designs a submarine for himself in order to visit the bottom of the sea. According to some tales he is not dead at all, but sleeping, until the world needs him again. He has never been forgotten.

The funeral carriage containing Alexander's gold coffin with his embalmed body inside, sets off on the long journey back to Macedonia. It was never to get there. Alexander's general, Ptolemy, persuaded the officer in charge to let him take the body to Egypt, where Ptolemy was ruler.

A fragment of Aristotelian philosophy found in an Egyptian papyrus. Alexander's conquests led to the expansion of Greek thought and culture throughout the Mediterranean and Near East.

DID HE LEAVE ANY LASTING LEGACY?

His conquests, and the Greek cities that he founded along his campaign routes led to the expansion of Greek culture far into central Asia. This expansion was supported and extended by the Greek kingdoms carved out by Alexander's successors from among his conquests. Under the Ptolemies, the dynasty of Greek kings and queens of Egypt founded by Ptolemy, Alexandria became the greatest city of the Mediterranean and a centre of Greek science and mathematics. Scholars came from all over the Greek world to study in its famous library.

A marble head of Ptolemy, Alexander's general, who became Ptolemy I of Egypt. He founded the Ptolemaic dynasty, which ended with the death of the famous Queen Cleopatra in 30 BC.

HOW DO WE KNOW SO MUCH ABOUT ALEXANDER?

Various people wrote histories of Alexander soon after his death. One of these was written by his friend Ptolemy, who went on to be king of Egypt. We do not have Ptolemy's book, but it was used by a later Roman historian named Arrian, whose account survives.

360 BC	355 BC	350 BC	345 BC	340 BC

**356 BC
BIRTH OF
ALEXANDER,
SON OF PHILIP II
OF MACEDONIA.**

ALEXANDER THE GREAT
KEY DATES

IMPORTANT DATES BEFORE 356 BC

1200 BC
Fall of Troy.

c. 800 BC
Homer writes the *Iliad*.

600 – 500 BC
Period of building of Greek colonies – spread of
Greeks throughout the Mediterranean.

c. 550 BC
Sparta, in the Greek Peloponnese, is the
most powerful city-state.

510 BC
Founding of the Roman Republic.

508 BC
Democratic government in Athens.

490–80 BC   Greece's Persian wars
– Persian invasions.

447 BC
Parthenon begun in Athens.
Golden age of Greek civilization.

431–404 BC
Peloponnesian war between Athens and Sparta.
Spartans victorious. Decline of Greek city-states.

358 BC
Macedonia in northern Greece unified by Philip II.

343 BC
Last Egyptian pharaoh defeated by the Persians.

IMPORTANT DATES AFTER 323 BC

305 BC
Alexander's generals found separate kingdoms:
Seleucus in Syria, Antigonus in Macedonia
and Ptolemy in Egypt.

102 BC
Birth of Julius Caesar.

86 BC
Romans capture Athens.

69 BC
Birth of Cleopatra, queen of Egypt.

44 BC
Julius Caesar assassinated.

31 BC
Antony and Cleopatra defeated at the
Battle of Actium.
Octavian becomes Augustus Caesar,
the first emperor of Rome.
Rome no longer a republic.

285 AD
Roman Empire split by Diocletian
into east and west.

324 AD
Constantine moves capital to Constantinople.

410 AD
Visigoths sack Rome.

1976 AD
Tomb of Philip II of Macedonia discovered
at Vergina.

340 BC	335 BC	330BC	325 BC	320 BC

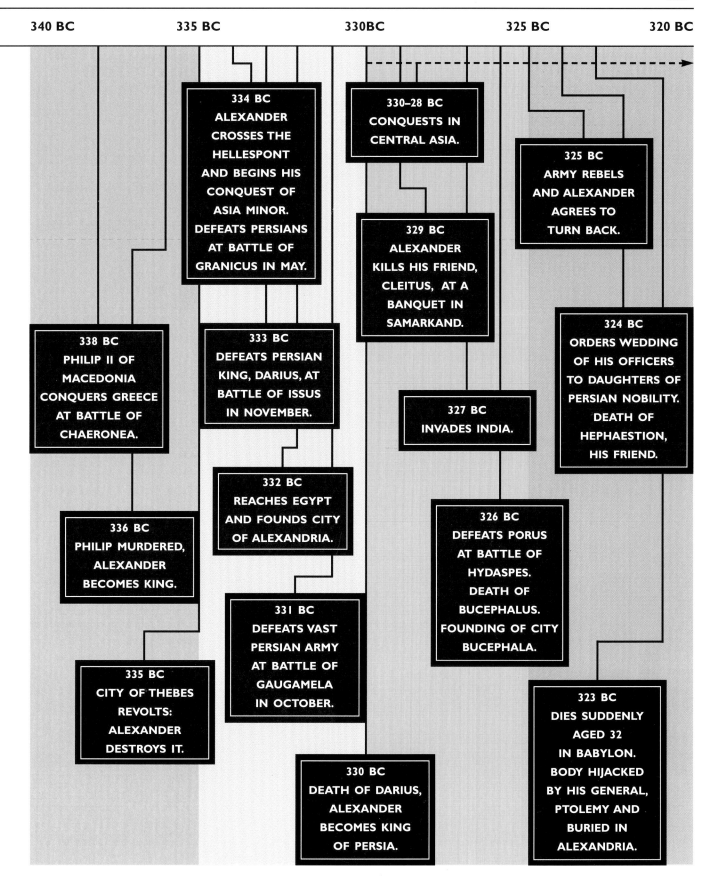

334 BC
ALEXANDER
CROSSES THE
HELLESPONT
AND BEGINS HIS
CONQUEST OF
ASIA MINOR.
DEFEATS PERSIANS
AT BATTLE OF
GRANICUS IN MAY.

330–28 BC
CONQUESTS IN
CENTRAL ASIA.

325 BC
ARMY REBELS
AND ALEXANDER
AGREES TO
TURN BACK.

329 BC
ALEXANDER
KILLS HIS FRIEND,
CLEITUS, AT A
BANQUET IN
SAMARKAND.

338 BC
PHILIP II OF
MACEDONIA
CONQUERS GREECE
AT BATTLE OF
CHAERONEA.

333 BC
DEFEATS PERSIAN
KING, DARIUS, AT
BATTLE OF ISSUS
IN NOVEMBER.

324 BC
ORDERS WEDDING
OF HIS OFFICERS
TO DAUGHTERS OF
PERSIAN NOBILITY.
DEATH OF
HEPHAESTION,
HIS FRIEND.

327 BC
INVADES INDIA.

332 BC
REACHES EGYPT
AND FOUNDS CITY
OF ALEXANDRIA.

336 BC
PHILIP MURDERED,
ALEXANDER
BECOMES KING.

326 BC
DEFEATS PORUS
AT BATTLE OF
HYDASPES.
DEATH OF
BUCEPHALUS.
FOUNDING OF CITY
BUCEPHALA.

331 BC
DEFEATS VAST
PERSIAN ARMY
AT BATTLE OF
GAUGAMELA
IN OCTOBER.

335 BC
CITY OF THEBES
REVOLTS:
ALEXANDER
DESTROYS IT.

323 BC
DIES SUDDENLY
AGED 32
IN BABYLON.
BODY HIJACKED
BY HIS GENERAL,
PTOLEMY AND
BURIED IN
ALEXANDRIA.

330 BC
DEATH OF DARIUS,
ALEXANDER
BECOMES KING
OF PERSIA.

GLOSSARY

ACHILLES The Greek hero who led his warriors into battle at the siege of Troy. The adventures of Achilles are told in HOMER'S *ILIAD*.

AMMON The Greek form of the name of the Egyptian god, Amun, king of the gods during the Ancient Egyptian empire. The Greeks identified him with their king of the gods, Zeus.

ARRIAN Greek historian writing at the time of the Roman emperor Hadrian. His book about Alexander is based upon the writings of Alexander's own historian, Callisthenes.

ARTEMIS The day of Alexander's birth was celebrated by the Greeks as being sacred to this Greek goddess of childbirth (known as Diana by the Romans). Later it was said that his birth coincided with the fire that destroyed the temple of Artemis at Ephesus, because she was away supervising his birth.

ATHENS Greek city-state. In the 5th century BC it was at the height of its power and prosperity and was a great centre of learning and art. Many famous Greeks lived there.

BARBARIAN Name given by the Greeks and Romans to people who they thought of as uncivilized and warlike.

BUCEPHALUS The name of Alexander's famous horse; this means 'ox-head' in Greek.

HERCULES In Greek mythology, a hero of superhuman strength.

HOMER The eighth-century Greek poet who wrote the *ILIAD* and the *Odyssey*. Very little is known about Homer but it is thought that he was blind.

ILIAD A story of epic adventure by the Greek poet HOMER, about a great city called Troy in Asia Minor, which was attacked by the Greeks. Greek soldiers managed to get inside Troy by a clever trick – they made a big wooden horse which they left outside the walls of the city. The inquisitive Trojans dragged the horse into the city and later that night Greek soldiers, hidden inside the horse, crept out and captured Troy.

PELOPONNESIAN WAR The war of 431 – 404 BC, fought and won by Sparta and its Peloponnesian allies against Sparta's rival, ATHENS. The war devastated the classical Greek world.

PHALANX The famous battle formation used by the Macedonian foot soldiers. They stood shoulder to shoulder with shields touching and long spears overlapping, in a compact block sometimes several rows deep.

PINDAR Greek poet who wrote poems and songs for cities and rulers throughout Ancient Greece. The Greeks counted him among their greatest poets.

PLUTARCH A Greek author best-known for his *Lives*; these were biographies of pairs of famous Greeks and Romans, such as Julius Caesar and Alexander.

SARCOPHAGUS A large, carved stone coffin to contain the bodies of the dead. Alexander's sarchophagus was made of solid gold.

SARISSA Long spear or lance used in the Macedonian PHALANX

TRIREME A long Greek warship with about 170 oars arranged in 3 decks. Its main weapon was an underwater ram at its base.

INDEX

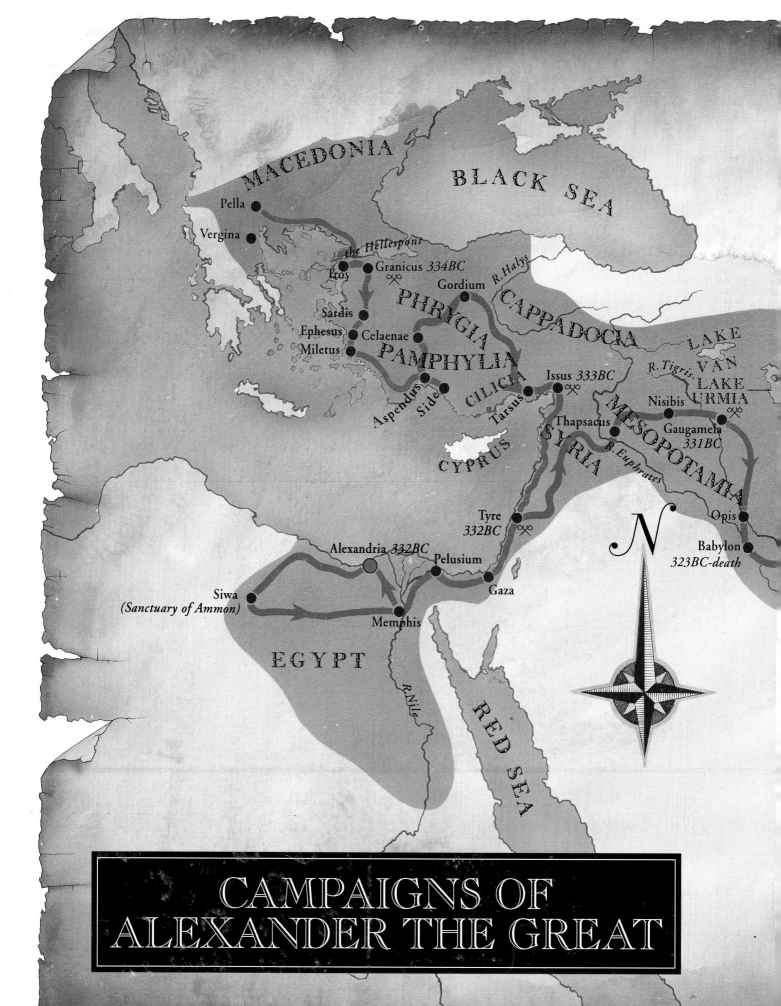

CAMPAIGNS OF ALEXANDER THE GREAT